PRIMARY SOURCES IN AMERICAN HISTORY™

THE HOMESTEAD ACT OF 1862

A PRIMARY SOURCE HISTORY OF THE SETTLEMENT OF THE AMERICAN HEARTLAND IN THE LATE 19TH CENTURY

JASON PORTERFIELD

The Rosen Publishing Group, Inc., New York

Published in 2005 by The Rosen Publishing Group, Inc.
29 East 21st Street, New York, NY 10010

Library of Congress Cataloging-in-Publication Data

Porterfield, Jason.
The Homestead Act of 1862: A primary source history of the settlement of the American heartland in the late 19th century/by Jason Porterfield.—1st ed.
    p. cm.—(Primary sources in American history)
Includes bibliographical references and index.
Contents: The vast frontier—Crossing the plains—The long trail—Settling down—Closing the frontier.
ISBN 1-4042-0178-5 (library binding)
1. Frontier and pioneer life—West (U.S.)—Juvenile literature. 2. Homestead law—West (U.S.)—History—19th century—Juvenile literature. 3. Public lands—West (U.S.)—History—19th century—Juvenile literature. 4. Land settlement—West (U.S.)—History—19th century—Juvenile literature. 5. West (U.S.)—History—Juvenile literature. [1. Frontier and pioneer life—West (U.S.) 2. Homestead law—West (U.S.) 3. Land settlement—West (U.S.) 4. West (U.S.)—History.]
I. Title. II. Series: Primary sources in American history (New York, N.Y.)
F596.P67 2005
978'.02—dc22

2003024434

Manufactured in the United States of America

On the front cover: John Bakken's sod house in Milton, North Dakota, circa 1895.

On the back cover: First row (left to right): John Bakken's sod house in Milton, North Dakota; Oswego starch factory in Oswego, New York. Second row (left to right): *American Progress*, painted by John Gast in 1872; the Battle of Palo Alto. Third row (left to right): Pony Express rider pursued by Native Americans on the plains; Union soldiers investigating the rubble of a Southern building.

CONTENTS

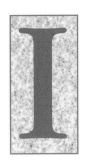NTRODUCTION

In 1862, Congress passed the Homestead Act to encourage settlement of America's prairies. States along the East Coast were densely populated, and waves of adventurers had crossed the continent to strike it rich on the West Coast. However, America's center remained unsettled by non-Native Americans. The congressmen who drafted the Homestead Act envisioned prosperous farms, towns, and ultimately states linking the coasts. The act offered settlers up to 160 acres (65 hectares) of land for only a small fee. In return, the settlers had to live on and improve the property.

LOOKING WESTWARD

People of all descriptions filed land claims and headed west in search of opportunity and adventure. Farmers searched for more fertile farms than the ones they had worked back east. City dwellers looked to escape overcrowding, epidemics, and poor living conditions. New immigrants, women, and freed African American slaves took advantage of the Homestead Act and the chance to own land for the first time.

Homesteaders did not find an easy life on the plains. They learned to deal with rock-hard soil, scorching summers, frigid winters, and isolation from family and friends. They battled drought, prairie fires, and even plagues of grasshoppers. Poverty and hardships did not stop them. One story describes a homesteader halting construction of his sod home until his wife could

This photograph shows a crowd of prospective homesteaders waiting to file claims at the land office in Perry, Oklahoma, on September 23, 1893. By 1904, approximately 720,000 farms totaling 100 million acres (40,469 ha) were established under the act. Homesteading continued at a pace of roughly 3 million acres (1.2 million ha) per year well into the 1930s.

sell her silk dress to raise money for a door and a window. Despite their sacrifices, many homesteaders did not see themselves as heroes. "[F]or the life of me I can't see anything heroic in coming out here to do farm work," homesteader Howard Ruede wrote to his family in Pennsylvania, as quoted in his collection of letters, *Sod-House Days*.

Today, many historians view the Homestead Act as a shining success that strengthened the country and provided a great opportunity for many Americans. Because of the act, millions of acres of prairie became prosperous farms. People who had never tried farming found themselves digging wells, building homes, and harvesting crops. The plains were integrated into the fabric of the country, and the territories became states within a few decades. The dream of one great nation extending across the continent came true.

TIMELINE

1607 —— Great Britain founds a colony at Jamestown, Virginia.

1763 —— Great Britain takes possession of French lands east of the Mississippi River.

1785 —— Congress enacts the Land Ordinance of 1785.

1787 —— Congress passes the Northwest Ordinance.

1803 —— The Louisiana Purchase is finalized.

1831–1832 —— American settlers travel the Oregon Trail for the first time.

1845 —— The United States annexes Texas.

1848 —— The United States acquires the California and New Mexico Territories from Mexico. Oregon becomes a U.S. territory.

1854 —— The Kansas-Nebraska Act allows settlement in the permanent Indian Territory.

1862 —— President Abraham Lincoln signs the Homestead Act into law.

TIMELINE

1863	The Homestead Act takes effect on January 1.
1867	Oliver Hudson Kelley founds the National Grange of the Patrons of Husbandry.
1869	The first transcontinental railroad is completed.
1873	Congress passes the Timber Culture Act.
1874	Grasshoppers ravage crops throughout the West. Joseph F. Glidden patents his design for barbed wire.
1893	The Cherokee Strip in the Oklahoma Territory opens for settlement.
1898	Congress opens the Alaska Territory to homesteaders.
1935	Congress withdraws the remaining public lands from homesteading.
1976	The Federal Land Policy and Management Act repealing the Homestead Act is passed.
1988	The last land title is granted under the Homestead Act.

CHAPTER 1

Great Britain founded the first successful settlement in America at Jamestown, Virginia, in 1607. For more than a century, Great Britain restricted its colonists to the territory east of the Appalachian Mountains. French and Spanish settlers, as well as Native American tribes, lived to the west.

THE VAST FRONTIER

A conflict between Great Britain and France over territory in the Great Lakes region led to the French and Indian War (1754–1763). Great Britain emerged victorious and gained all of France's territory east of the Mississippi River, except New Orleans. After the war ended, many British settlers sought to move west.

The British parliament decided to limit settlement west of the mountains. It feared that too many settlers in the frontier could cause problems with Native Americans or the Spanish. Parliament authorized only wealthy individuals and land companies to own property in the West.

This map of the United States was created by John Melish in 1816. At the time, the nation was comprised of eighteen states and possessed close to a million square miles (2.6 million sq kilometers) of unorganized territories. Between 1816 and 1862, when the Homestead Act was passed, the United States acquired a significant amount of additional land through war and diplomacy and by direct purchase.

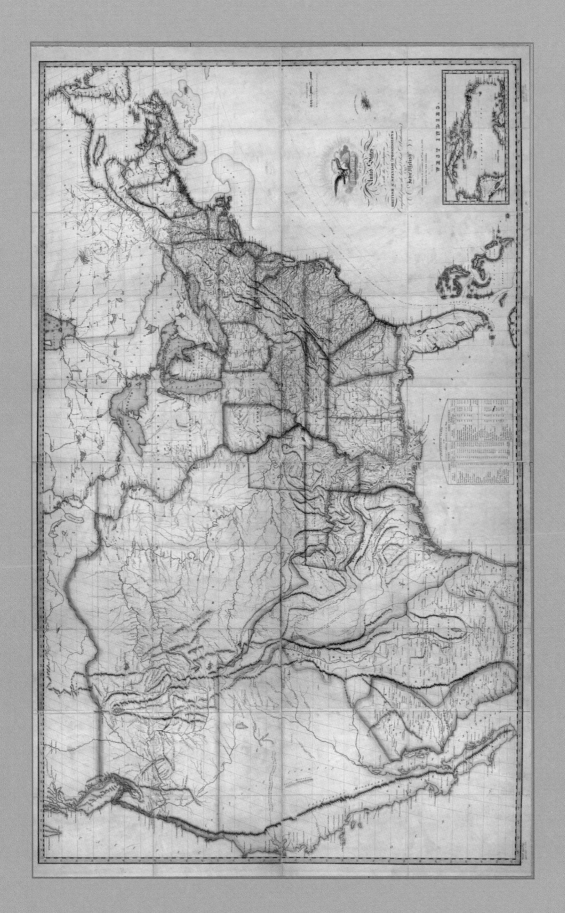

9

Many colonists ventured into the wilderness anyway. Some followed the explorer Daniel Boone through present-day Kentucky and into the Ohio River valley. They settled on land that would become the states of Kentucky, West Virginia, and Tennessee. Other pioneers defied the law and moved into the Northwest Territory, an area around the Great Lakes north of the Ohio River and east of the Mississippi. Still more settled in the French-controlled Mississippi River valley.

Western settlers opposed Britain's restrictions on land ownership in the West. When American colonists began calling for independence from Great Britain, they promised to loosen rules on who could legally own land in the West. This pledge prompted many people on the frontier to join the American Revolution (1775–1783) on the colonial side. At the close of the war in 1783, the new United States of America consisted of the territory of the original thirteen colonies, plus all British-owned territories lying between the Appalachian Mountains and the Mississippi River.

The Northwest Ordinance

Following the end of the American Revolution, settlers began pouring across the mountains. Many headed to the Northwest Territory. Virginia, Connecticut, New York, and Massachusetts all claimed different sections of the territory. They based their ownership claims on their original colonial charters, which gave vague instructions relating to their boundaries.

The remainder of the states resented these claims. They felt that the federal government should control the territory. The United States had fallen deeply into debt in order to fight the American Revolution. If the federal government owned the Northwest Territory, it could sell plots of land to prospective settlers, thereby

Daniel Boone was involved in the exploration and settlement of the western frontier for nearly seventy years. In 1775, he founded the town of Boonesborough (now Boonesboro) in present-day Kentucky. Three years later, he was captured by Shawnee Indians, who gave him the name Shel-tow-ee, or Big Turtle. He escaped in time to warn the town of a planned Shawnee attack. This portrait of Boone was created by Alonzo Chappel in 1861.

generating funds for paying off its debt. The four states agreed to give up their claims on the territory. By 1786, it had all come under the control of the government, creating a public domain.

The federal government immediately recognized the need to improve the administration of the Northwest Territory. Settlers in the frontier were dissatisfied by attempts to govern settlements from faraway East Coast capitals. They wanted to make their own laws. They demanded a system for establishing towns, building roads, and entering the Union as states. Some threatened to leave the United States and establish their own nation if their demands were not met.

Congress sought to answer the frontiersmen's demands with the Northwest Ordinance. A congressional committee drew up the bill over the course of a week in July 1787. At this time, Congress was still operating under the Articles of Confederation, the document that governed the country before the writing of the Constitution. Eight states unanimously adopted the Northwest Ordinance on July 13, 1787. The document would come to serve as a template for the establishment of every subsequent state in the Union.

The Northwest Ordinance called for the Northwest Territory to be governed as one district, later to be formed into three to five states, the boundaries of which would be set by Congress. In the early stages, territories would be managed by a governor, a secretary, and three judges, all selected by Congress. Once the population reached "five thousand free male inhabitants of full age," each territory would establish an elected representative body and a council appointed by the governor. A territory could become a state once it met certain population requirements. According to the Northwest Ordinance:

> And, whenever any of the said States shall have sixty thousand free inhabitants therein, such State shall be admitted, by its delegates, into the Congress of the United States, on an equal footing with the original States in all respects whatever, and shall be at liberty to form a permanent constitution and State government.

The new state governments had to follow the guidelines contained in the Articles of Confederation. Other provisions in the Northwest Ordinance established public education, guaranteed free passage on all rivers in the area, and forbade slavery within the territory.

The Northwest Ordinance proved very successful in easing the territories into statehood. Surveyors divided the territory into townships drawn from a standardized geographic baseline running west from the Ohio River. Each township contained 6 square miles (16 sq km). The townships were then divided into thirty-six sections of land of 640 acres (259 ha) each.

An earlier document, the Land Ordinance of 1785, had created an orderly system for settlement within the territories. Operating under the Land Ordinance and the Northwest Ordinance, settlers slowly moved into the Northwest Territory. They were drawn by the low cost of land: $1.25 per acre ($3.09 per ha). Five states eventually emerged from the Northwest Territory. Ohio came first, in 1803, followed by Indiana in 1816, Illinois in 1818, Michigan in 1837, and finally Wisconsin in 1848.

The Louisiana Purchase

The growth of farms and townships in the Northwest Territory created a need for a convenient shipping route. Most river networks in the area drained into the Mississippi River. With access to the Mississippi River, farmers and craftsmen in the territories could ship their goods south all the way to the Gulf of Mexico. But traffic on the river was controlled by French colonists based in the important port of New Orleans.

President Thomas Jefferson sent a delegation to Paris in 1803 to negotiate a deal that would allow the United States to purchase New Orleans. French emperor Napoléon Bonaparte offered instead to sell the United States all of the Louisiana Territory for $15 million. The delegation accepted the offer and signed the Louisiana Purchase on May 2, 1803. The Louisiana Purchase added 828,000 square miles (2,144,510 sq km) of land between the

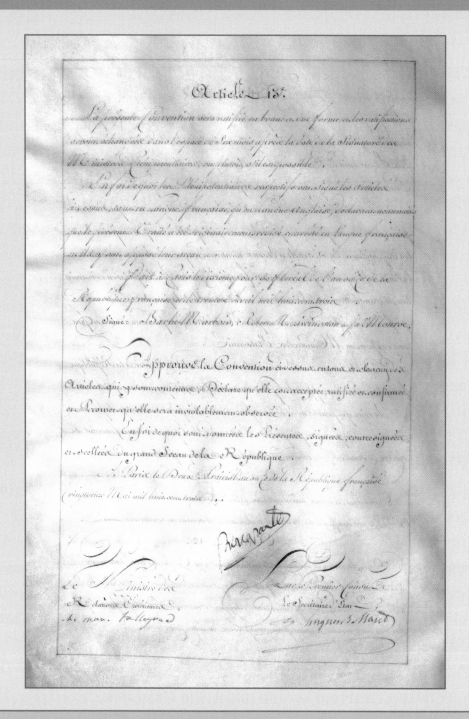

This is a page from the Louisiana Purchase treaty between the United States and France. In addition to outlining the financial and territorial components of the transaction, the treaty specified that the United States would extend citizenship to French and Spanish inhabitants of the Louisiana Territory. It made no reference to the roughly 150,000 Native Americans living there. Refer to page 55 for a partial transcript of the Louisiana Purchase treaty.

Mississippi River and the Rocky Mountains and doubled the size of the United States. In a letter to statesman James Dickenson on August 9, 1803, Jefferson expressed his delight over the purchase. As quoted in *The Writings of Thomas Jefferson,* he wrote:

> The acquisition of New Orleans would of itself have been a great thing, as it would have ensured to our western brethern the means of exporting their produce: but that of Louisiana is unappreciable, because, giving us the sole dominion of the Mississippi, it excludes those bickerings with foreign powers, which we know of a certainty would have put us at war with France immediately; and it secures to us the course of a peaceable nation.

Jefferson immediately set to work asserting the United States' claim to the Louisiana Territory. He commissioned a small party of men, led by Meriwether Lewis and William Clark, to explore the new territory, establish alliances with Native American tribes, and search for a water route to the Pacific Ocean.

Lewis and Clark began their journey on the Missouri River, leaving St. Louis on May 14, 1804, with a party of forty-five men. Guided by a Shoshone woman named Sacagawea, who joined the expedition in present-day North Dakota, they came in sight of the Pacific Ocean on November 7, 1805. After spending the winter in Oregon, they began making their way back the next spring. The Lewis and Clark expedition returned to St. Louis on September 23, 1806, a little more than two years after setting out.

Though its members did not find a waterway from the Missouri to the Pacific, the expedition's reports of friendly tribes, vast prairies, and woodlands full of game caused a sensation. "The

At the time of his selection to lead the expedition into the Louisiana Territory, Meriwether Lewis *(left)* was a captain in the United States Army and President Jefferson's trusted secretary. His partner, William Clark *(right)*, was also an army officer, as well as a skilled surveyor and mapmaker. They led a team of forty-five men, known as the Corps of Discovery, which included Clark's slave York. The expedition lasted approximately twenty-eight months, from May 14, 1804, to September 23, 1806.

portion of the continent watered by the Missouri and [its] branches from the Cheyenne upward is richer in beaver and otter than any country on streams lying within the Rocky Mountains," wrote Meriwether Lewis, as quoted in *The Letters of the Lewis and Clark Expedition.* Rugged explorers and trappers read his words and began filtering into the territory to seek their fortune.

CHAPTER 2

The lure of the West, which drew trappers and explorers toward the Rocky Mountains, soon began working on farmers and businessmen. Accounts of Lewis and Clark's journey described lush farmlands as well as forests and rivers full of game. Some men saw great potential in the Oregon Territory, a large area containing the present-day states of Oregon and Washington, as well as parts of Montana, Wyoming, Idaho, and some of British Columbia, Canada. Dissatisfied with life in the East, many dreamed of a new beginning in Oregon.

CROSSING THE PLAINS

The Oregon Frontier

At the beginning of the nineteenth century, the United States and Great Britain both claimed the Oregon Territory. Each nation had claims going back to the late eighteenth century. As they vied for control of a thriving fur market, companies of both nations established trading posts. They signed a treaty calling for "joint occupation" of Oregon in 1818. However, the British dominated the region by 1828, with a self-supporting base at Fort Vancouver.

A few Americans worried that their country would miss the chance to settle in the area. According to Sanford Wexler in *Westward Expansion*, as early as 1820, a congressman from

Fort Vancouver was the massive British outpost on the banks of the Columbia River in present-day Washington. It served as the administrative center and main supply depot for Britain's Hudson Bay Company, which ran a profitable fur trading business in the Oregon Territory in the early nineteenth century. In violation of British regulations, the fort's manager, John McLoughlin, welcomed American settlers and provided them with essential supplies during the 1830s and 1840s.

Virginia named Dr. John Floyd suggested that Congress create a committee to "inquire into the situation of the settlements upon the Pacific Ocean and the expediency of occupying the Columbia River." Floyd headed the committee, which issued a glowing review of the territory's agricultural potential. He drafted a bill calling for the annexation of Oregon in 1823. However, many in Congress lacked his vision, and the bill was defeated.

Despite Congress's reluctance to take over the territory, people back east considered privately settling there. Many, however, dismissed the trip as unrealistic. The most common route to

Oregon was a long sea voyage around South America. People traveling this way could expect to pay the huge sum of $300 (about $5,200 today) to spend six months sailing the 13,000 miles (20,922 km) through the dangerous waters of Cape Horn.

In 1831, an icemaker from Cambridge, Massachusetts, named Nathaniel J. Wyeth began organizing an expedition of traders to Oregon. He and thirty-one others intended to make the trip overland, bypassing the ocean voyage. Starting from Independence, Missouri, the group crossed Kansas and Nebraska, following the Platte River into southern Wyoming and through a break in the Rocky Mountains called South Pass. From there, the route crossed Idaho, following the Snake River until it joined with the Columbia, which the group followed to Fort Vancouver. They arrived in Oregon in October 1832, seven months after leaving Massachusetts. Wyeth's successful crossing of the continent inspired others to do the same. He had successfully brought the first immigrants over the Oregon Trail. With an overland route opened, "Oregon fever" swept the country.

Farmers headed to Oregon to escape falling prices for their crops. People living in cities sometimes left to get away from outbreaks of deadly epidemics, such as cholera, typhoid, and dysentery. They thought fleeing the cities could keep them healthy, but many immigrants died of these diseases on the trail. Still others left to get away from the debate over slavery, escaping to a land where there were no slaves. Whatever their reasons, the number of pioneers traveling the 2,000 miles (3,219 km) of the Oregon Trail kept increasing, from 1,000 in 1843, to 4,000 in 1844, and more. The American population in the territory grew so quickly that Great Britain relinquished its claim in 1846, and Oregon officially became a U.S. territory in

This illustration by W. H. Jackson portrays a wagon train at Barlow Cutoff, a shortcut along the Oregon Trail. As time passed, settlers developed alternate routes instead of following the original trail all the way along the south bank of the Columbus River. By doing so, the settlers shaved as much as a week off travel time. Nevertheless, the settlers were in constant fear of being attacked by Indians. Barlow Cutoff is near Mount Hood, Oregon.

1848. Settlers kept arriving, with a peak of 55,000 people traveling on the trail in 1850. By 1869, about 350,000 people had taken the Oregon Trail.

The Annexation of Texas

While much of the country was catching Oregon fever, Americans at the southern end of the Mississippi River valley eyed Mexico-owned Texas. Mexico had declared its independence from Spain in 1821. Previously closed to American settlement and trade, the new nation opened its doors to both.

This painting shows Mexicans and Texans fighting to the death during the battle of the Alamo, the most famous battle of the Texas Revolution. By the end of the battle, Mexican forces had killed all 189 of the Texans defending the Alamo. This defeat motivated other Texans to continue their struggle for independence. The phrase "Remember the Alamo" became a battle cry in future battles between Texas and Mexico.

Traders and settlers entered via the Santa Fe Trail, which extended 800 miles (1,287 km) from Independence, Missouri, to Santa Fe, New Mexico. Most people traveled by wagon trains, with settlers banding together to assist each other along the way. In 1830, so many Americans lived in Texas that the Mexican government forbade further American settlement.

By 1835, enough Americans had settled in Texas to agitate for its separation from Mexico, beginning with the Texas Revolution that fall. The battle of the Alamo in San Antonio, Texas, on March 6, 1836, inspired the independence movement. After enduring a twelve-day siege, 189 Americans fought to the death against an army of 4,000 Mexican soldiers. The revolution ended a little more than a month later, and Texas became independent. The same year, the Mexican territory of California also declared independence.

Americans saw Texas's independence as an easy means to expand the nation's territory. Planters and farmers in the far south saw annexation as a way to acquire more or better land, as northerners were doing in the Northwest Territory. In 1836, settlers in the Republic of Texas requested that the United States annex Texas.

Some settlers bitterly opposed annexation, fearing it would anger Mexico and result in war. Others were afraid it would lead to the creation of more states that allowed slavery, which had been prevented in the Old Northwest (another name for the Northwest Territory). The Texans withdrew their request later that year, but the annexation debate continued. In a speech to Congress on January 16, 1838, Congressman John Quincy Adams declared, "I do believe slavery to be a sin before the sight of God and that is the reason why we should not annex Texas to the Union," as quoted in *John Quincy Adams: A Personal History of an Independent Man,* by Marie B. Hect.

The pro-annexation faction eventually won, and President John Tyler signed a resolution to annex Texas on March 1, 1845. The resolution stated that no more than four additional states could emerge from the territory. On December 29, 1845, Texas became the twenty-eighth state. A series of tense border encounters between the American and Mexican armies followed, with Congress finally declaring war on May 13, 1846.

The Mexican-American War ended on September 17, 1847, when the Mexican president, General Antonio López de Santa Anna, surrendered Mexico City to the United States. Under the Treaty of Guadalupe Hidalgo, signed on February 2, 1848, the United States set the boundary between Texas and Mexico at the Rio Grande. Mexico also ceded the territories of California and New Mexico, totaling 1.2 million square miles (3.1 million sq km), to the United States in return for $15 million. The United States had once again nearly doubled its territory.

Gold in California

Just days before the Treaty of Guadalupe Hidalgo officially made California a U.S. territory, a workman named James Marshall discovered flakes of gold at John Sutter's mill in California's lower Sacramento Valley. Sutter tried to keep his find a secret, but word spread quickly. Thousands of people poured into California, hoping to strike it rich.

Gold hunters had to choose between either a long and expensive sea voyage or a grueling overland trip through often inhospitable country. Some chose to follow the Oregon Trail to Idaho, turning southward there and descending into northern California. Others took trails across scorching deserts and over steep mountains into the southern end. By the end of 1849, more than 100,000 people had settled in California. The territory gained statehood in October 1850.

Opening the Prairie

The rapid growth of the nation and the population's drift toward the Pacific created a problem for the United States. Although the land east of the Missouri River was densely populated and settlers continued to flock toward California and Oregon, much of the territory in between remained empty of settlements. California was then cut off from the other states by a vast expanse of desert, mountains, and prairie.

The territory, however, was not uninhabited. Native American tribes made their homes throughout the region. The U.S. government had even pushed some tribes into this "great American desert." In 1825, Congress created an official Indian Territory in present-day Kansas and Oklahoma, to push tribes off desirable land in the East. President Andrew Jackson took the issue a step further by signing the Indian Removal Act in 1830, relocating eastern tribes onto land west of the Mississippi. Nine years later, the government forced the Cherokee, Choctaw, Chickasaw, Creek, and Seminole tribes from their lands, marching them to Oklahoma along what became known as the Trail of Tears.

By the 1850s, Congress was willing to forget about the "permanent Indian Territory" in the interest of creating more public land to sell. Stephen Douglas, a senator from Illinois, wished to open the Indian Territory for settlement. His Kansas-Nebraska Act of 1854 divided the territory into a Kansas Territory and a Nebraska Territory. The settlers in each territory would decide if they wanted to allow slavery. The bill passed, and settlers began entering Kansas.

These settlers claimed property under the Preemption Act of 1831. Under this law, a settler could stake a claim to 160 acres

This is the text from President Andrew Jackson's "On Indian Removal" message to Congress. In it, Jackson strongly advocated relocating eastern Native American tribes to land west of the Mississippi River. Jackson delivered the message in December 1830, a little more than six months after Congress had passed the Indian Removal Act. As a result of the act, thousands of Indians died as they were forcibly relocated by the U.S. military. The involuntary journey west became known as the Trail of Tears. Refer to pages 55–56 for a partial transcription.

uncommitted to any other course than the strict line of constitutional duty; and that the securities for this independence may be rendered as strong as the nature of power and the weakness of its possessor will admit, — I cannot too earnestly invite your attention to the propriety of promoting such an amendment of the constitution as will render him ineligible after one term of service.

It gives me pleasure to announce to Congress that the benevolent policy of the government, steadily pursued for nearly thirty years in relation to the removal

(65 ha) of land. After living on it for a year, the settler could buy the land for $1.25 per acre ($3.09 per ha). The act had helped to settle the Northwest Territory, but many politicians and settlers saw it as flawed. Congress sought a better way to distribute public lands in the future.

The Homestead Act

In 1862, while the country was fighting the Civil War, Congressman Galusha A. Grow addressed the issue of how to settle the prairie in a way that was fair to all by sponsoring a bill in Congress called the Homestead Act. The Homestead Act promised 160 acres (65 ha) of free land to "any person who is

HR 125

Thirty-seventh

Congress of the United States,

At the Second Session

BEGUN AND HELD AT THE CITY OF WASHINGTON

in the District of Columbia

on Monday the second day of December one thousand eight hundred and sixty-one

AN ACT to secure homesteads to actual settlers on the public domain.

Be It Enacted by the Senate and House of Representatives of the United States of America in Congress assembled,

That any person who is the head of a family, or who has arrived at the age of twenty-one years, and is a citizen of the United States, or who shall have filed his declaration of intention to become such, as required by the naturalization laws of the United States, and who has never borne arms against the United States government or given aid and comfort to its enemies, shall from and after the first January, eighteen hundred and sixty-three be entitled to enter one quarter section or a less quantity of unappropriated public lands, upon which said person may have filed a pre-emption claim, or which may, at the time the application is made, be subject to pre-emption at one dollar and twenty-five cents, or less, per acre; or eighty acres or less of such unappropriated lands, at two dollars and fifty cents per acre; to be located in a body, in conformity to the legal subdivisions of the public lands, and after the same shall have been surveyed: Provided, That any person owning and residing on land may, under the provisions of this act, enter other land lying contiguous to his or her said land, which shall not, with the land so already owned and occupied, exceed in the aggregate, one hundred and sixty acres.

Sec. 2. And be it further enacted, That the person applying

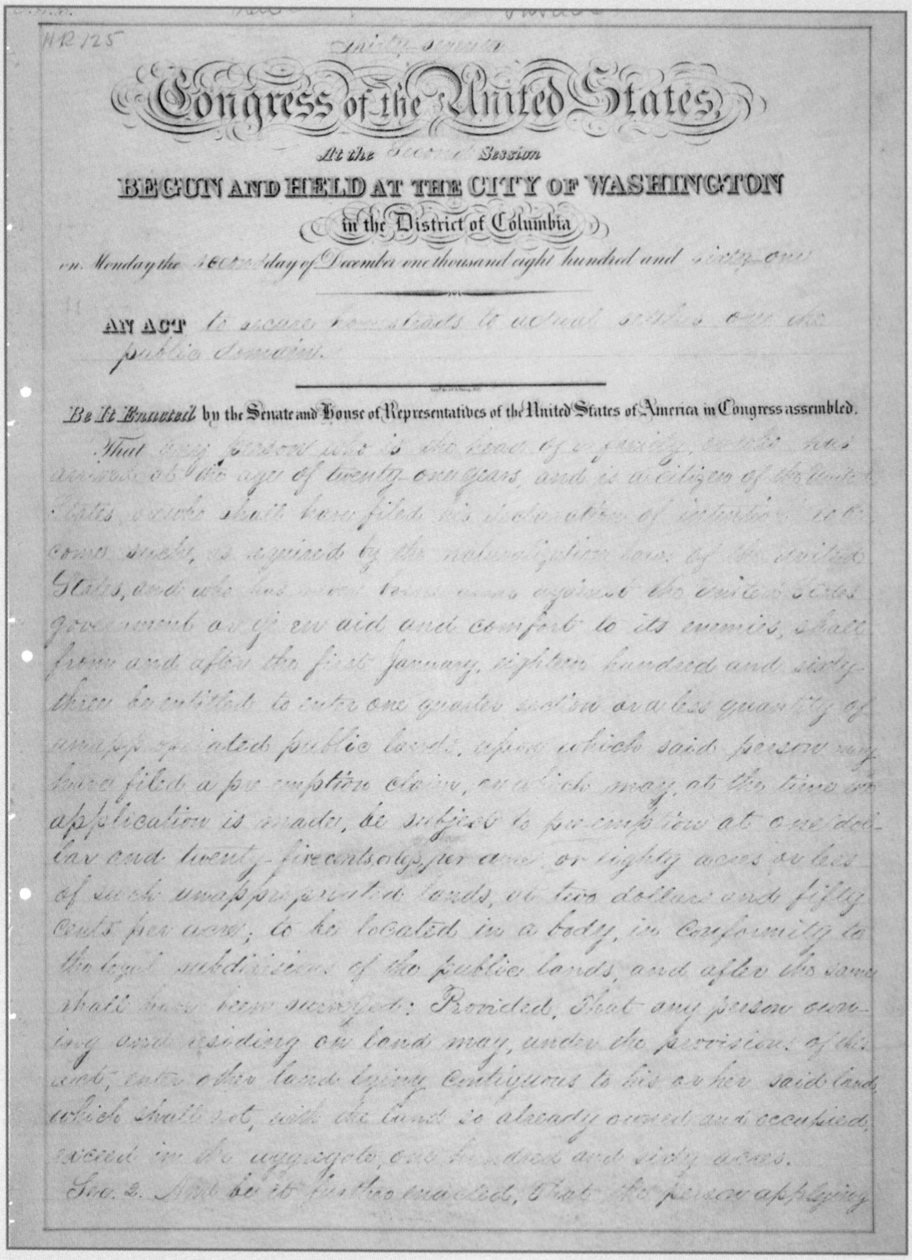

The Homestead Act, the first page of which is shown here, was passed by Congress on May 20, 1862. Enacted during the Civil War, it excluded Confederate soldiers. After the war, Union soldiers were allowed to deduct time served from the law's residency requirements. The legislation was not written very well—a reality that led dishonest speculators and ranchers to defraud the homestead program. Congress later made several revisions to close the law's loopholes. Refer to page 56 for a partial transcription.

the head of a family, or who has arrived at the age of twenty-one years, and is a citizen of the United States, or who shall have filed his declaration of intention to become one." The settler had only to pay a filing fee.

In return for the land, the settler had to live on it and farm it for five years. Several earlier attempts to pass similar bills had failed in Congress. Most Southern politicians opposed free land in the West, fearing it would lead to the creation of more states that opposed slavery. With most Southern states having seceded from the Union before the start of the Civil War, the bill passed easily and went into effect on January 1, 1863. The Homestead Act applied to land in all but the original thirteen states, plus Kentucky, Tennessee, Vermont, Maine, Texas, and West Virginia. Over the next three decades, the Homestead Act would have a vast effect on the country's development.

CHAPTER 3

THE LONG TRAIL

In the late hours of December 31, 1862, a long line waited for the land office in Brownville, Nebraska, to open. The crowd waited impatiently to file claims for free land under the Homestead Act the instant it went into effect. Most anxious was a thirty-six-year-old soldier named Daniel Freeman. On furlough for the holidays, he had to return to the army on January 1. Others took pity on Freeman and allowed him to go to the front of the line. Legend has it that Freeman filed the first homestead claim in the United States just after midnight on January 1, 1863.

The scene in front of the Brownville Land Office became a common one throughout the West. The government set up land offices in towns and villages to handle the claims that poured in whenever a territory opened for settlement. Lines of people waiting to stake their claims sometimes became so dense that the land office clerks used ladders to second-story windows to get into their offices. No one seemed to mind that much of the free land was dry prairie.

This photograph of Daniel Freeman was taken around 1904 when the first homesteader was about seventy-eight years old. He is shown here standing, holding a gun, with a hatchet tucked into his belt. Freeman settled in Beatrice, Nebraska, in 1863.

Within six months of the Homestead Act's passage, 224,500 acres (90,852 ha) were claimed in Kansas and Nebraska alone.

The Call for Settlers

Newspapers and advertisements throughout the East proclaimed the need for settlers. The respondents came from all walks of life. Many homesteaders were already experienced farmers. They moved west with their families, looking for better land. Others came from the cities and had much to learn about farming.

Under the Homestead Act, women were just as free to register a claim for a homestead as were men. Many free-spirited, adventurous women headed west to own property. After the Civil War, widows of Union soldiers staked claims, wishing to make a fresh start and provide for their families. An amendment to the Homestead Act reduced the time these widows had to live on the claim before "proving up." In order to become the legal landowner, a settler had to prove up to the land office, usually after five years of living on the claim, providing official evidence that he or she occupied and had made improvements to the land. In *Letters of a Woman Homesteader*, Elinore Pruitt Stewart, who homesteaded in Oklahoma in the 1890s, wrote that "any woman who can stand her own company, can see the beauty of the sunset, loves growing things, and is willing to put in as much time at careful labor as she does over the washtub, will certainly succeed; will have independence, plenty to eat all the time, and a home of her own in the end."

Freed African American slaves also took advantage of the Homestead Act. Rather than move to Northern cities or remain in the South where they were harshly mistreated, many opted to stake out their own land. In 1870, a former slave named Robert Anderson became the first African American homesteader in

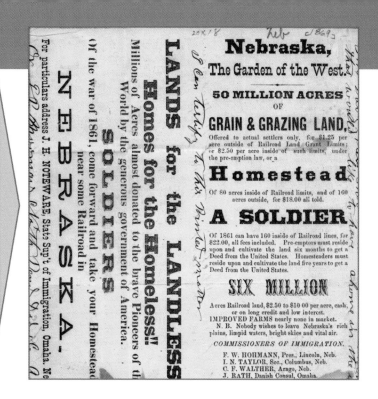

The broadside at right was published by the Nebraska State Department of Immigration in 1869. Aimed at Civil War veterans, it announces the special rate for former Union soldiers and touts Nebraska as "the Garden of the West." Advertisements like this were published across the West.

Nebraska. There were only 689 other African Americans in the state at the time. Within the next twenty years, the number rose to 8,900. Another former slave, Benjamin "Pap" Singleton, brought thousands of African Americans west to Kansas. They settled and homesteaded around a town named Nicodemus, established in 1877 on a former homestead of 160 acres (65 ha). Between 1877 and 1879, a record 20,000 African Americans left the South for Kansas. This massive exodus earned them the nickname exodusters.

When the Oklahoma Territory was opened to settlement in 1889, an African American businessman named Edwin P. McCabe bought 320 acres (130 ha), intending it to serve as a population center for homesteading African Americans. He named the town Langston, after John Mercer Langston, the first African American congressman elected to Congress from Virginia. Other communities of African Americans flourished throughout the West, as more and more of them sought opportunity in the territories.

New immigrants to the United States seized the chance to own land in their new country. Some states and territories even

Before taking advantage of the Homestead Act, Benjamin "Pap" Singleton *(left)* urged blacks to acquire farmland in his native Tennessee. However, it soon became clear that whites would not sell them productive land there. Therefore, in 1874, Singleton and his associates founded the Edgefield Real Estate and Homestead in Tennessee. It monitored the migration of more than 20,000 blacks to Kansas between 1877 and 1879. A family of African American homesteaders in Nicodemus, Kansas, is shown in the photograph at right.

advertised in other countries, hoping to attract more people. "Land for the Landless! Homes for the Homeless!" offered one flier from the Nebraska State Department of Immigration. Earlier immigrants encouraged their countrymen to homestead, describing life on the plains and offering advice. In the pioneer guide *Emigrant Life in Kansas*, Englishman Percy Ebbutt recommended:

> You must make up your mind to rough it. You must cultivate
> the habit of sleeping in any kind of surroundings, on a

board and without a pillow, indoors or out. I have been to sleep on horseback before now. Learn to ride as soon as you possibly can; a man or boy who cannot ride is, in a new country, about as valuable as a clerk who cannot write in a city office.

People from all over Europe descended on the West. So many Swedish and Norwegian immigrants arrived in Minnesota during the late 1860s that an editor of the *St. Paul Pioneer* remarked: "It seems as if the Scandinavian Kingdoms were being emptied into the state," according to Huston Horn in *The Old West: The Pioneers.* As long as they became citizens or intended to do so, and as long as they improved their claims, people from all over the world were welcome to their 160 acres (65 ha).

Setting Out for the Prairie

In the early years of the Homestead Act, settlers relied on wagons to get to their new land. They learned lessons about packing from their predecessors, the settlers who had crossed the country on the Oregon Trail.

Most chose farm wagons for the journey, as these were durable, versatile, and easy to handle. Large wagons, such as the famous Conestogas, were top-heavy and tended to tip over in rough terrain. Settlers stored tools in boxes built into the underside of the wagon. Spare parts such as axles, wheels, and wagon tongues were strapped to the sides. Many people converted open wagons by covering them with canvas or durable cloth treated with linseed oil to make it waterproof. Sturdy hickory boughs fixed to the wagon's sides supported the covers. The covers could be drawn up to allow ventilation for passengers.

The Chrisman sisters—from left to right, Hattie, Lizzie, Lutie Bell, and Jennie Ruth—pose by a sod house in Custer County, Nebraska, in 1886. Between 1887 and 1892, the sisters filed separate homestead claims. Unfortunately for the youngest, Jennie Ruth, all the land was gone by the time she was eligible to file. Many single women filed homestead claims. They often put off marriage to ensure that the land would be titled to them.

The flapping white covers resembled sails, giving the wagons the nickname prairie schooners.

Inside the wagon, settlers packed food first. Eggs, grain, coffee and heavily salted bacon were essential, as they would all keep for a long time when properly stored. Tools needed for clearing land and farming, such as axes, hammers, plows, and ropes, also went into the wagon. Clothing, bedding, and cooking utensils followed. Some travelers made extra room for a few luxuries, such as furniture, books, and musical instruments. By the time everything was packed, there was barely room for passengers!

Teams of mules or oxen pulled most wagons. Mules were nimble and smart, and they moved quickly. On the other hand, oxen cost less, were better tempered, and ate almost any type

This 1886 photograph shows a family posing by their horse-drawn wagon in Loup Valley, Nebraska. The search for good homesteads was often a frustrating experience, especially for families like this one with small children. Families lived and traveled in wagons until they secured their land claims.

of plant. Most settlers chose oxen, even though they were much slower than mules. Horses, far more expensive than either, were generally saved for riding.

Relatively few homesteaders had to endure long overland routes like those on the journeys of the pioneers who had gone to California or Oregon. By the 1880s, railroads crossed much of the prairie. Homesteaders needed only a ticket to the town of their choice. From there they could usually buy equipment and supplies.

Staking the Claim

Once they arrived at their destination, homesteaders had to select a claim and file it at the land office. The best claims, those with good soil and plentiful water, were usually the first to be chosen. Valleys were highly desirable, as they provided shelter from the ceaseless prairie winds.

Upon finding a suitable piece of uninhabited land, the homesteader rushed to the land office to file the claim. Otherwise, another settler might beat him or her to the claim. The land offices were often at least 40 to 60 miles (64 to 97 km) away. Settlers found ways to keep others away until they could complete the journey. They might start digging a well and plowing a few furrows before going to the land office. These signs of habitation often held off other land hunters for a few days.

Once at the land office, the homesteader had the claim checked, ensuring that no one else had already filed for the desired land. This was done by checking the survey coordinates of the land in question. If the land was already claimed, the settler either went looking for a new spot or gave up. If the claim went through, then the new homesteader paid a $10 fee to settle the land temporarily and a $2 commission to the land agent. With the application and the receipt in hand, the new homesteader was ready to begin the backbreaking task of improving the land.

CHAPTER 4

Homesteading required hard work, dedication, and sacrifice. Settlers put in long hours of toil turning the wild prairie into farmland. They coped with the bad weather and natural disasters typical of the plains. Only the barest materials were available for building, and water was usually scarce. "We wanted to be in a free state, but I reckon there ain't no freedom here except to die of thirst," wrote a Kansas homesteader before giving up his claim, according to Sanford Wexler in *Westward Expansion.* Some homesteaders gave up, heading back to their old lives in the East. Most of them stuck with their claims, however, turning them into prosperous farms.

SETTLING DOWN

Proving Up

After filing a claim, a settler had five years to prove up to the land office in order to keep the land. Even experienced farmers who moved onto the plains were not prepared for the difficulties of proving up. The problems began with the soil itself. Across the prairie, the top layer was sod, hard-packed soil so densely laced with grass roots that a normal plow could not break through. Homesteaders earned the nickname sodbusters because they had to break through the sod in order to plant anything. Some farmers did this with axes. Others used a

This 1908 photograph shows a homesteader turning over sod with a horse-drawn grasshopper plow. Equipment such as the grasshopper plow was crucial to the successful development of a homestead claim. Homesteaders were called sodbusters. At first, the nickname was applied as a slur, but it came to embody the hardy nature of the settlers who eventually tamed the land.

grasshopper plow, a cast-steel plow invented by John Deere in 1837. It was designed specifically to bite into and turn sod. Special steel plowshares kept the sod from gumming up the plow. They resembled a grasshopper's wings, earning the plow its name.

Building a home presented another challenge. Except for those on the river valleys on the eastern prairie, there were no trees on the plains. Settlers were forced to make do with the only building materials at hand: the long strips of sod cut from the ground by the grasshopper plows. These strips were between 12 and 18 inches (30 to 46 centimeters) wide. The homesteader cut them into 2- or 3-foot (0.6- to 1-meter) lengths with an ax and hauled them to the building site, often a small hill that had been dug out. The strips were placed with the grass side down, staggered like brickwork in three rows side by side. The walls of an average sod house were more than 3 feet (1 m) thick! Rods driven down through the corners helped to secure the sod in place. Frames for doors and windows were set into the walls. When the walls were tall enough, settlers constructed the roof. The rafters of the roof were reinforced with boards, poles, or brush, depending on what the family could afford. These were covered by a layer of prairie grass. A layer of sod finished off the roof. The floor usually remained hard-packed earth.

Sod houses had many advantages. Their thick walls made them easy to heat in the winter and kept them cool during the hot summer months. Strong winds could not blow them over. They would not burn down under any circumstances. And, of course, they were very cheap to build. All of the sod needed for a house could be taken from a half acre (0.2 ha) of land. Neighbors often got together to help each other build these homes in "building bees."

Their faults, however, were glaring. Sod houses were impossible to keep clean. Some settlers hung cheesecloths from the rafters to catch the silt that sifted down from the ceiling. During rainstorms, sod house roofs leaked horribly and sometimes collapsed. No matter how well sealed the walls were, unwanted guests such as mice, snakes, and insects always found a way inside.

This certificate, dated January 20, 1868, made Daniel Freeman the legal owner of the land he had claimed five years earlier. It was issued after Freeman submitted the required proof that he had improved the land. Freeman listed a stable, a corn crib, forty apple trees, and about 400 peach trees among the improvements he had made.

As Kansas homesteader Howard Ruede wrote in *Sod-House Days: Letters From a Kansas Homesteader, 1877–78*, a person did not need a dog "in order to have plenty of fleas, for they are natives too and do their best to drive out the intruding settlers. Just have a dirt floor and you have fleas sure. They seem to spring from the dust of the earth." Some homesteaders grew to love their "soddies," but most rejoiced when they could finally afford to buy the lumber to build a frame house.

Finding water proved problematic for most homesteaders on the dry plains. Some lucky settlers could depend on nearby creeks or rivers. Others collected rainwater in barrels and cisterns. Most dug wells, sometimes digging more than 200 feet (61 m) by hand before hitting water. They used windmills to pump the water to the surface. These windmills pumped hundreds of gallons of water per day, providing water for livestock and crops. In the arid high plains, farmers had to learn new techniques that used less water. They planted their crops on terraces dug into hills. Resembling giant steps, the terraces collected rainwater, instead of allowing it to run downhill. Farmers also learned to irrigate, pumping water to their crops from a distant source. Once homesteaders had a home and a water supply, they only had to work the fields and endure life on the prairie until the land became theirs.

Cheating the Homestead Act

Some homesteaders were less than honest in filing their claims. Many of these people were land speculators hoping to acquire free land and then sell it to someone else for a profit. Some of them filed multiple claims under false names. Others had homesteads in several different states. Families occasionally lied about their children's ages, saying they were twenty-one so that they could file additional claims to increase the families' land holdings.

Another trick involved filing a claim around another unclaimed patch of land. By enclosing the other land with their own, dishonest homesteaders could gain the use of the surrounded property without anyone noticing. Other inventive people sought ways to dodge the Homestead Act's requirement that they build a house on the land. Some constructed houses on wheels that could be rolled from one claim to the next. Others noticed that the act called for a "house measuring 12 by 12." The instructions did not specify if that meant feet or inches. The dishonest homesteaders built tiny houses measuring 12 inches by 12 inches (31 by 31 cm) and then reported that they had built a "12 by 12" house. From the Homestead Act's enactment, countless dishonest people got away with filing fraudulent claims.

Hardship on the Prairie

Hard work and sheer determination helped homesteaders overcome obstacles such as a lack of water and building materials. Still, the prairie's climate often created problems that no amount of hard work could dispel. Droughts came in the summer, accompanied by searing 100° Fahrenheit (38° Celsius) temperatures. Livestock suffered and crops withered and died in such heat. Heavy hailstorms occasionally battered the plains, sometimes wrecking whole fields. During the winters, temperatures dropped far below freezing, as low as -30°F (-34°C). Sudden blizzards could bury a farm under several feet of snow.

In the autumn, when the grass became dry, prairie fires swept across the landscape. They often started as a result of lightning or the embers of an untended campfire. Such fires could destroy a farmer's livelihood in minutes. Farmers fought them by digging fire lines, lighting backfires designed to burn toward the prairie fire and consume its fuel, and smothering the flames with wet blankets or piles of dirt. If the fire proved too strong, the homesteader rushed animals and everything of value into the fireproof sod house. Huddled there, the homesteader and family would be safe from the fire, even as their crops burned.

Taken by Solomon D. Butcher around 1900, this photograph shows Ephraim Swain Finch demonstrating how he attempted to kill grasshoppers on his homestead in Nebraska during the plague of 1876. (Butcher drew grasshoppers onto the picture with India ink.) Grasshopper plagues swept across Nebraska between 1873 and 1878. Many farmers lost their crops. In response, the federal government furnished the farmers with seed loans.

Throughout the 1870s, farmers had to endure plagues of locusts and grasshoppers invading the plains. In 1874, swarms of grasshoppers rampaged across the prairie, eating everything in sight. According to Wexler, a Nebraska farmer named Addison E. Sheldon observed them at work:

As far as the eye could reach in every direction the air was filled with them. Where they alighted they covered the

Under the Timber Culture Act of 1873, anyone who qualified for a homestead could claim an additional 160 acres (65 ha) of land provided that he or she plant 40 acres (16 ha) of trees and care for them for ten years. The law was intended to increase the supply of wood, increase rainfall, and moderate climate extremes. However, the law was a dismal failure. Land speculators took advantage of loopholes in the act, and little permanent tree growth resulted. The Timber Culture Act was repealed in 1891.

ground like a heavy crawling carpet. Growing crops disappeared in a single day. Trees were stripped of leaves. Potatoes, turnips and onions were pursued into the earth. Clothing and harness were cut into shreds if left exposed.

The grasshoppers ruined farmers across the West. As the air grew cooler that year, the grasshoppers disappeared as suddenly as they had arrived.

More minor difficulties constantly assailed farmers. Cattlemen taking their cattle to market often drove their herds right through farmers' fields. Crop prices were always uncertain, and the prices charged by railroads for shipping crops to markets always seemed too high. Though Native Americans seldom caused any trouble for the homesteaders, many settlers lived in fear of them.

Even when things went well, it was sometimes difficult to make a living on only 160 acres (65 ha). Later land acts made it easier for homesteaders to own more land. The Timber Culture Act of 1873 allowed any homesteader to apply for another 160 acres (65 ha) if at least one-fourth of it would be planted in trees within four years. Settlers could also still acquire land through the Preemption Act of 1831. With hard work and patience, honest farmers could own a homestead claim and increase their land holdings.

When five years had passed, the time came to prove up. The homesteader went to the land office to give evidence that the obligations had been fulfilled. Two witnesses gave testimony that all of the conditions had been met. If the evidence was satisfactory, the homesteader paid a $4 fee. He or she received a patent for the land in return, making ownership of the homestead official.

CHAPTER 5

CLOSING THE FRONTIER

As the nineteenth century drew to a close, the rhythms of life on a homestead remained much the same. During the spring and summer, the homesteaders planted and raised their crops. They harvested with the coming of autumn. Over the winter, they mended equipment and cared for livestock. When not working, settlers relaxed with their families or got together with neighbors. Communities organized quilting bees and dances held in barns.

More and more people came to the West, and towns began to form. Regions began holding fairs, where people competed in contests ranging from shooting and horseracing to baking and canning. Carnivals, circuses, and medicine shows toured growing Western communities, bringing a sense of wonder to the lives of hardened farm families.

People gathering at such events would look at the crowds and marvel. The vast territories had become populated. Towns thrived where there had once been empty prairie. Roads replaced dusty trails. Railroads and telegraph lines crisscrossed

At right is Joseph Glidden's patent for barbed wire. It includes a sketch and what it describes as a "full, clear, and exact description of the construction and operation" of the wire. As Glidden envisioned, barbed wire proved quite valuable to homesteaders in preventing cattle from breaking through fences and destroying crops.

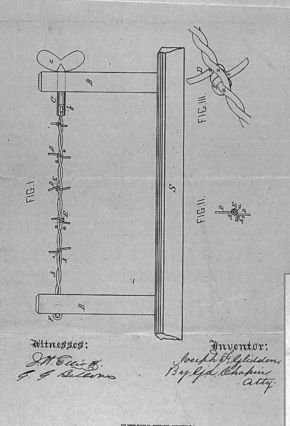

J. F. GLIDDEN.
Wire-Fences.

No. 157,124.

Patented Nov. 24, 1874.

Witnesses:

J. H. Elliott
G. G. Belsons

Inventor:

Joseph F. Glidden
By G. L. Chapin
Atty.

UNITED STATES PATENT OFFICE.

JOSEPH F. GLIDDEN, OF DE KALB, ILLINOIS.

IMPROVEMENT IN WIRE FENCES.

Specification forming part of Letters Patent No. 157,124, dated November 24, 1874; application filed October 27, 1873.

To all whom it may concern:

Be it known that I, JOSEPH F. GLIDDEN, of De Kalb, in the county of De Kalb and State of Illinois, have invented a new and valuable Improvement in Wire Fences; and that the following is a full, clear, and exact description of the construction and operation of the same, reference being had to the accompanying drawings, in which—

Figure 1 represents a side view of a section of fence exhibiting my invention. Fig. 2 is a sectional view, and Fig. 3 is a perspective view, of the same.

This invention has relation to means for preventing cattle from breaking through wire fences; and it consists in combining, with the twisted fence-wires, a short transverse wire, coiled or bent at its central portion about one of the wire strands of the twist, with its free ends projecting in opposite directions, the other wire strand serving to bind the spur-wire firmly to its place, and in position, with its spur ends perpendicular to the direction of the fence-wire, lateral movement, as well as vibration, being prevented. It also consists in the construction and novel arrangement, in connection with such a twisted fence-wire, and its spur-wires, connected and arranged as above described, of a twisting key or head-piece passing through the fence-post, carrying the ends of the fence-wires, and serving, when the spurs become loose, to tighten the twist of the wires, and thus render them rigid and firm in position.

In the accompanying drawings, the letter B designates the fence-posts, the twisted fence-wire connecting the same being indicated by the letter A. C represents the twisting key, the shank of which passes through the fence-post, and is provided at its end with an eye, *b*, to which the fence-wire is attached. The outer end of said key is provided with a transverse thumb-piece, *c*, which serves for its manipulation, and at the same time, abutting against the post, forms a shoulder or stop, which prevents the contraction of the wire from drawing the key through its perforation in said post.

The fence-wire is composed at least of two strands, *a* and *s*, which are designed to be twisted together after the spur-wires have been arranged in place.

The letter D indicates the spur-wires. Each of these is formed of a short piece of wire, which is bent at its middle portion, as at E, around one only of the wire strands, this strand being designated by the letter *a*. In forming this middle bend or coil several turns are taken in the wire, so that it will extend along the strand-wire for a distance several times the breadth of its diameter, and thereby form a solid and substantial bearing-head for the spurs, which will effectually prevent them from vibrating laterally or being pushed down by cattle against the fence-wire. Although these spur-wires may be turned at once around the wire strand, it is preferred to form the central bend first, and to then slip them on the wire strand, arranging them at suitable distances apart. The spurs having thus been arranged on one of the wire strands are fixed in position and place by approaching the other wire strands *s* on the side of the bend from which the spurs extend, and then twisting the two strands *a s* together by means of the wire key above mentioned, or otherwise. This operation locks each spur-wire at its allotted place, and prevents it from moving therefrom in either direction. It clamps the bend of the spur-wire upon the wire *a*, thereby holding it against rotary vibration. Finally, the spur ends extending out between the strands on each side, and where the wires are more closely approximated in the twist, form shoulders or stops *s*, which effectually prevent such rotation in either direction.

Should the spurs, from the untwisting of the strands, become loose and easily movable on their bearings, a few turns of the twisting key will make them firm, besides straightening up the fence-wire.

What I claim as my invention, and desire to secure by Letters Patent, is—

A twisted fence wire having the transverse spur-wire D bent at its middle portion about one of the wire strands *a* of said fence-wire, and clamped in position and place by the other wire strand *s*, twisted upon its fellow, substantially as specified.

JOSEPH F. GLIDDEN.

Witnesses:
G. L. CHAPIN,
J. H. ELLIOTT.

the countryside, and fences broke up the plains where livestock had once roamed free.

Fencing the Prairie

The arrival of more neighbors forced many homesteaders to fence in their property, keeping their livestock close to home and away from other people's crops. Since traditional fencing materials such as split rails and stones were scarce in many places, settlers turned to a farming innovation. In 1874, Joseph F. Glidden received a patent for barbed wire. Glidden's design consisted of two pieces of wire twisted together and held together by intermittent knots with sharp protruding ends.

Homesteaders welcomed the invention of barbed wire, as it was inexpensive and easy to put up. The fences that the homesteaders erected kept their own horses and cattle in their pastures and away from the crops. Cattle ranchers, however, hated the new invention. For decades they had driven their cattle to market over unfenced prairie, even through homestead claims. The new fences blocked access to watering holes and pastures along their routes. In some places, violent disputes broke out between the fence-building homesteaders and the cattle drivers.

Still, ranchers who grazed their animals on the ever-shrinking public domain saw the end of their way of life looming. "It will very soon be cheaper to fence than to herd stock," wrote cattle rancher James Brisbin in his 1881 book, *The Beef Bonanza; or, How to Get Rich on the Plains*. Brisbin also quoted fellow rancher David Sherwood:

"It is absolutely necessary to own a large part of your range, especially the waterfront, so as to keep out sheepmen, settlers, and other cattle owners . . . Government lands, where watering places exist are fast becoming occupied by settlers and colonies, and very soon the opportunity for locating large ranches will entirely disappear."

Farmers who did not concentrate on raising livestock fenced in their crops, usually corn, oats, or wheat. Crops thrived as agricultural advances increased the productivity of the fields. In 1874, Russian immigrants developed a new kind of wheat. The hardy grain could withstand the severe weather conditions found on the plains. New farm machinery, such as reapers and combines pulled by lumbering steam-powered tractors, allowed homesteaders to cultivate more land in less time than before. The prairie was well on its way to becoming one of the most productive agricultural regions in the world.

Civilizing the Prairie

A woman homesteading in Montana during the 1880s named Nannie T. Alderson recorded her reasons for staying in the West in *A Bride Goes West*:

The West was very tolerant toward the lesser faults of human conduct. It was even willing to overlook the greater if they were not repeated. A man's past was not questioned, nor a woman's either; the present was what counted. A man could even be known as wanted by the law elsewhere, yet this was not held against him here so long as he showed a willingness to walk the straight path. Half the charm of the country for me was its broad-mindedness. I loved it from the first.

By the 1890s, the incredible distances that had kept Western settlements isolated and helped Westerners remain anonymous had disappeared. Railroads and telegraph lines knit these communities together. After Samuel Morse sent the first public telegram in 1844, the telegraph became a popular way to deliver messages quickly over long distances. The invention brought news and a means of instant communication to once-isolated prairie towns. The first transcontinental telegraph extended from Washington, D.C., to San Francisco, California. "The Pacific to the Atlantic sends greetings; and may both oceans be dry before a foot of all the land that lies between them shall belong to any other than one united country," read the first message sent over the line, on October 22, 1861, as quoted in Sanford Wexler's *Westward Expansion.*

The first transcontinental railroad was completed at Promontory Summit in the Utah Territory on May 10, 1869. New settlers used the railroads for their initial journey west and to ship their produce to markets.

Settlers and farmers had been stubbornly self-reliant and suspicious of organizations, as well as separated by geographic distances. However, they began breaking through their social isolation. As railroads raised shipping rates and prices for farm products dropped, farmers began banding together for economic survival. This movement, called the Granger Movement, began with Oliver Hudson Kelley's founding of the National Grange of the Patrons of Husbandry in 1867. The organization sought to aid farmers by persuading lawmakers to pass laws regulating railroad rates.

Poor homesteaders were often forced to take out loans for purchasing equipment. They became indebted to banks, railroads, and

A boisterous crowd participates in the ceremony celebrating the joining of the tracks of the Union Pacific Railroad and the Central Pacific Railroad at Promontory Summit, Utah, on May 10, 1869. During the ceremony, one train from the East and one from the West stopped within several feet of each other and a spike made of an alloy of gold and copper was driven into the connecting tracks. The completion of the intercontinental railroad made it easier for prospective homesteaders to travel west in search of claims.

other big moneylenders. The Granger movement encouraged farmers to save their own money and make purchases outright. Many Western towns and villages had grange halls, where farmers could meet and discuss their business. Local granges established stores for members and built grain elevators and mills for members' own use. The political power of the granges waned as other organizations such as the Populist Party and the Greenback Party became the political voices of the farmers. Still, the granges remained important social networks for farmers for many years.

Oliver Hudson Kelley was commissioned by President Andrew Johnson in 1866 to survey agricultural conditions in the South. He was alarmed by the generally inefficient agricultural practices that he witnessed. The following year, he founded the National Grange of the Patrons of Husbandry, which served as both an institutional organization, a cooperative society, and a national social network for farmers. Under Kelley's leadership, the National Grange attracted close to 270,000 dues-paying members in its first seven years.

Towns became increasingly important to farmers as the nineteenth century drew to a close. The grange halls drew them to town for monthly meetings. Their children walked to town every day to attend school. Cattle and crops were sent to town to be shipped by railroads to larger towns and cities. The post office collected and sent mail. Mills, blacksmith shops, and general stores served the needs of homesteaders. Wexler quoted an anonymous North Dakota pioneer describing the changes:

"Language cannot exaggerate the rapidity with which these communities are built up. You may stand ankle deep in the short grass of the uninhabited wilderness; next month a mixed train will glide over the waste and stop at some point where the railroad has decided to locate a town. Men, women, and children will jump out of the cars and their chattels will be tumbled out after them. From that moment the building begins."

The days when a farmer might have to ride for days to reach a post office were essentially over.

Statehood and the Frontier's End

By the early 1890s, many of the Western territories had acquired enough citizens to become states. Iowa, Colorado, Montana, Utah, and other plains territories became states by 1896.

In 1891, the United States purchased land in Oklahoma from the Western Band of the Cherokee Indians. The land was called the Cherokee Strip, and the government opened it to homesteaders in 1893. It was the last land made available to settlers in the continental United States. Oklahoma became the forty-sixth state in 1907, followed by New Mexico and Arizona in 1912. Statehood had come to the last of the Western territories. The Homestead Act remained in effect in some regions until 1935, when the government withdrew the remaining public lands from homesteading. Settlers seeking free land had to look elsewhere.

Potential homesteaders turned to the Alaska Territory. The United States had purchased the vast piece of land from Russia in 1867 for $7.2 million. Gold strikes and the timber and fur industries attracted a few hearty adventurers to the enormous wilderness, but most of the territory's 615,230 square miles (1,593,438 sq km) remained unsettled. Congress opened the territory to homesteading in 1898, hoping to encourage settlement. Alaska became the forty-ninth state on January 3, 1959. Its borders remained opened to homesteaders for nearly twenty years.

Congress's passage of the Federal Land Policy and Management Act in 1976 repealed the Homestead Act, though it allowed a ten-year exception to Alaska. In 1974, a veteran from California named Kenneth Deardorff filed a claim for 80 acres (32 ha) of land in Alaska. Though he satisfied all of the requirements by 1979, he did not receive a title to the land until 1988. The paperwork's delay officially made Kenneth Deardorff the last person to acquire land under the Homestead Act.

In the years between Daniel Freeman's filing for his claim in Nebraska in 1863, and Kenneth Deardorff's land patent in 1988, more than 2 million people took advantage of the Homestead Act. They arrived in search of opportunity, and their stories of taming the prairies have become the stuff of American folk-lore. Homesteaders settled more than 250 million acres (101 million ha) throughout the United States. Their hard work turned what was once uncultivated land into some of the most productive farming country in the world.

PRIMARY SOURCE TRANSCRIPTIONS

Page 14: Excerpt from the treaty concerning the Louisiana Purchase

Transcription

The President of the United States of America and the First Consul of the French Republic in the name of the French People desiring to remove all Source of misunderstanding relative to objects of discussion mentioned in the Second and fifth articles of the Convention of the 8th Vendémiaire on 9/30 September 1800 relative to the rights claimed by the United States in virtue of the Treaty concluded at Madrid the 27 of October 1795, between His Catholic Majesty & the Said United States, & willing to Strengthen the union and friendship which at the time of the Said Convention was happily reestablished between the two nations have respectively named their Plenipotentiaries to wit The President of the United States, by and with the advice and consent of the Senate of the Said States; Robert R. Livingston Minister Plenipotentiary of the United States and James Monroe Minister Plenipotentiary and Envoy extraordinary of the Said States near the Government of the French Republic; And the First Consul in the name of the French people, Citizen Francis Barbé Marbois Minister of the public treasury who after having respectively exchanged their full powers have agreed to the following Articles.

Article I
Whereas by the Article the third of the Treaty concluded at St Ildefonso the 9th Vendémiaire on 1st October 1800 between the First Consul of the French Republic and his Catholic Majesty it was agreed as follows.

His Catholic Majesty promises and engages on his part to cede to the French Republic six months after the full and entire execution of the conditions and Stipulations herein relative to his Royal Highness the Duke of Parma, the Colony or Province of Louisiana with the Same extent that it now has in the hand of Spain, & that it had when France possessed it; and Such as it Should be after the Treaties subsequently entered into between Spain and other States.

And whereas in pursuance of the Treaty and particularly of the third article the French Republic has an incontestible title to the domain and to the possession of the said Territory—The First Consul of the French Republic desiring to give to the United States a strong proof of his friendship doth hereby cede to the United States in the name of the French Republic for ever and in full Sovereignty the said territory with all its rights and appurtenances as fully and in the Same manner as they have been acquired by the French Republic in virtue of the above mentioned Treaty concluded with his Catholic Majesty.

Page 25: Excerpt from President Andrew Jackson's "On Indian Removal" speech

Transcription

It gives me pleasure to announce to Congress that the benevolent policy of the Government, steadily pursued for nearly thirty years, in relation to the removal of the Indians beyond the white settlements is approaching to a happy consummation. Two important tribes have accepted the provision made for their removal at the last session of Congress, and it is believed that their example will induce the remaining tribes also to seek the same obvious advantages.

The consequences of a speedy removal will be important to the United States, to individual States, and to the Indians themselves. The pecuniary advantages which it promises to the Government are the least of its recommendations. It puts an end to all possible danger of collision between the authorities of the General and State Governments on account of the Indians. It will place a dense and civilized population in large tracts of country now occupied by a few savage hunters. By opening the whole territory between

Tennessee on the north and Louisiana on the south to the settlement of the whites it will incalculably strengthen the southwestern frontier and render the adjacent States strong enough to repel future invasions without remote aid. It will relieve the whole State of Mississippi and the western part of Alabama of Indian occupancy, and enable those States to advance rapidly in population, wealth, and power. It will separate the Indians from immediate contact with settlements of whites; free them from the power of the States; enable them to pursue happiness in their own way and under their own rude institutions; will retard the progress of decay, which is lessening their numbers, and perhaps cause them gradually, under the protection of the Government and through the influence of good counsels, to cast off their savage habits and become an interesting, civilized, and Christian community.

Page: 26: Excerpt from the Homestead Act of 1862

Transcription

Be it enacted by the Senate and House of Representatives of the United States of America in Congress assembled, That any person who is the head of a family, or who has arrived at the age of twenty-one years, and is a citizen of the United States, or who shall have filed his declaration of intention to become such, as required by the naturalization laws of the United States, and who has never borne arms against the United States Government or given aid and comfort to its enemies, shall, from and after the first of January, eighteen hundred and sixty-three, be entitled to enter one quarter section or a less quantity of unappropriated public lands, upon which said person may have filed a preemption claim, or which may, at the time the application is made, be subject to preemption at one dollar and twenty-five cents, or less, per acre; or eighty acres or less of such unappropriated lands, at two dollars and fifty cents per acre, to be located in a body, in conformity to the legal subdivisions of the public lands, and after the same shall have been surveyed: Provided, That any person owning and residing on land may, under the provisions of this act, enter other land lying contiguous to his or her said land, which shall not, with the land so already owned and occupied, exceed in the aggregate, one hundred and sixty acres.

Section 2. And be it further enacted, That the person applying for the benefit of this act shall, upon application to the register of the land office in which he or she is about to make such entry, make affidavit before the said register or receiver that he or she is the head of a family, or is twenty-one years or more of age, or shall have performed service in the army or navy of the United States, and that he has never borne arms against the Government of the United States or given aid and comfort to its enemies, and that such application is made for his or her exclusive use and benefit, and that said entry is made for the purpose of actual settlement and culti-vation, and not either directly or indirectly for the use or benefit of any other person or persons whomsoever; and upon filing the said affidavit with the register or receiver, and on payment of ten dollars, he or she shall thereupon be permitted to enter the quantity of land specified: Provided, however, That no certificate shall be given or patent issued therefor until the expiration of five years from the date of such entry; and if, at the expi-ration of such time, or at any time within two years thereafter, the person making such entry; or, if he be dead, his widow; or in case of her death, his heirs or devisee; or in the case of a widow making such entry, her heirs or devisee, in the case of her death; shall prove by two credible witnesses that he, she, or they have resided upon or cultivated the same for the term of five years immediately succeeding the time of filing the affidavit afore-said, and shall make affidavit that no part of said land has been alienated, and he has borne true allegiance to the Government of the United States; then, in such case, he, she, or they, if at that time a citizen of the United States, shall be entitled to a patent, as in other cases provided for by law: And, provided, further, That in case of the death of both father and mother, leaving an infant child, or children, under twenty-one years of age, the right and fee shall enure to the benefit of said infant child or children; and the executor, administrator, or guardian may, at any time within two years after the death of the surviving parent, and in accordance with the laws of the State in which such children for the time being have their domicil, sell said land for the benefit of said infants, but for no other purpose; and the purchaser shall acquire the absolute title by the purchase, and be entitled to a patent from the United States, on payment of the office fees and sum of money herein specified.

Approved, May 20, 1862.

GLOSSARY

annex To incorporate territory into an existing political unit, such as a country or a state.

Articles of Confederation The first constitution of the United States, drafted by the original thirteen colonies. They remained in effect from 1781 to 1788.

brethern Brothers; used especially in formal address. Spelled "brethren" in contemporary English.

charter A document outlining the principles, functions, and organization of a corporate body; a constitution.

cholera An acute infectious disease of the small intestine, often fatal, caused by contaminated food or water.

Conestoga wagon A large, broad-wheeled wagon designed for hauling freight across soft soil.

dysentery A painful intestinal disease.

emigrant A person who leaves his or her home country to settle in another.

exodus A mass departure.

frontier A wilderness just beyond or at the edge of a settled area of a country.

furlough A leave of absence, especially from military duty.

immigrant A person who enters and permanently settles in a foreign country.

irrigate To supply dry land with water by means of ditches, pipes, or streams.

ordinance A rule established by authority, such as a statute or a regulation.

preemption The right to purchase something before others, especially the right to purchase public land that is granted to one who has settled on that land.

silt   Very fine particles of earth or mud.

surveyor   One who determines the boundaries, area, or elevations of land or geographic features by measuring angles and distances.

telegraph   An apparatus that transmits messages over long distances through coded electrical signals.

Trail of Tears   The forced march in 1838 of more than 18,000 Cherokee and other Native Americans from their homes in the East to Oklahoma. More than 4,000 died during the trip.

transcontinental   Spanning across a continent.

typhoid   An infectious intestinal disease caused by contaminated food or water, characterized by symptoms such as high fever, headache, and intestinal hemorrhaging.

unanimously   Of one mind; without dissent.

OR MORE INFORMATION

Homestead National Monument of America
8523 West State Highway 4
Beatrice, NE 68310
(402) 223–3514
Web site: http://www.nps.gov/home/homestead_act.html

The Jefferson National Expansion Memorial
11 North 4th Street
St. Louis, MO 63102
(314) 655–1700
e-mail: jeff_superintendent@nps.gov
Web site: http://www.nps.gov/jeff/main.htm

Web Sites

Due to the changing nature of Internet links, the Rosen Publishing Group, Inc., has developed an online list of Web sites related to the subject of this book. This site is updated regularly. Please use this link to access the list:

http://www.rosenlinks.com/psah/haei

FOR FURTHER READING

Duncan, Dayton. *People of the West.* New York: Little, Brown, and Company, 1996.

Ketchum, Liza. *Into a New Country: Eight Remarkable Women of the West.* New York: Little, Brown, and Company, 2000.

Patent, Dorothy Hinshaw. *The Lewis and Clark Trail: Then and Now.* New York: Dutton Children's Books, 2002.

Schlissel, Lillian. *Black Frontiers: A History of African American Heroes in the Old West.* New York: Simon & Schuster, 1995.

Stefoff, Rebecca. *The Oregon Trail in American History.* Berkley Heights, NJ: Enslow Publishers, 1997.

Wilder, Laura Ingalls. *Little House on the Prairie.* New York: HarperTrophy, 1973.

# BIBLIOGRAPHY

Adams, Alexander B. *The Disputed Lands: A History of the American West.* New York: G. P. Putnam's Sons, 1981.

Alderson, Nannie T. *A Bride Goes West.* New York: Farrar and Rinehart, 1942.

Billington, Ray Allen. *Westward Expansion: A History of the American Frontier.* New York: Macmillan, 1967.

Brisbin, James S. *The Beef Bonanza; or, How to Get Rich on the Plains.* Norman, OK: University of Oklahoma Press, 1959.

Dick, Everett. *The Sod-House Frontier 1854–1890.* Lincoln, NE: Johnsen Publishing Company, 1954.

Ebbutt, Percy G. *Emigrant Life in Kansas.* New York: Arno Press, 1975.

Ferris, Robert G., ed. *The National Survey of Historic Sites and Buildings, Vol. XI.* Washington, DC: United States Department of the Interior, National Park Service, 1963.

Hect, Marie B. *John Quincy Adams: A Personal History of an Independent Man.* New York: Macmillan, 1972.

Horn, Huston. *The Old West: The Pioneers.* New York: Time-Life Books, 1974.

Hough, Emerson. *The Passing of the Frontier.* New Haven, CT: Yale University Press, 1918.

Hulbert, Archer Butler, ed. *The Oregon Crusade: Across Land and Sea to Oregon.* Denver: Stewart Commission of Colorado College and Denver Public Library, 1935.

Jackson, Donald, ed. *The Letters of the Lewis and Clark Expedition, with Related Documents.* Chicago: University of Illinois, 1962.

Jefferson, Thomas. *The Writings of Thomas Jefferson.* P. L. Ford., ed. New York: Putnam, 1891.

Jones, Mary Ellen, ed. *The American Frontier: Opposing Viewpoints.* San Diego, CA: Greenhaven Press, Inc., 1994.

Kreyche, Gerald F. *Visions of the American West.* Lexington, KY: University Press of Kentucky, 1989.

Merk, Frederick. *History of the Westward Movement.* New York: Alfred A Knopf Inc., 1978.

Noy, Gary, ed. *Distant Horizon: Documents from the Nineteenth-Century American West.* Lincoln, NE: University of Nebraska Press, 1999.

Olson, James C. *History of Nebraska.* Lincoln, NE: University of Nebraska Press, 1966.

Paden, Irene D. *The Wake of the Prairie Schooner.* New York: American Book-Stratford Press, Inc., 1943.

Rhodes, James Ford. *History of the United States from the Compromise of 1850.* New York: Harper and Brothers, 1893.

Ruede, Howard. *Sod-House Days: Letters From a Kansas Homesteader, 1877–78.* John Ise, ed. New York: Columbia University Press, 1937.

Stewart, Elinore Pruitt. *Letters of a Woman Homesteader.* Lincoln, NE: University of Nebraska Press, 1961.

Torr, James D., ed. *The American Frontier.* San Diego, CA: Greenhaven Press, Inc., 2002.

United States National Park Service. *Prospector, Cowhand, and Sodbuster.* Washington, DC: United States Department of the Interior, National Park Service, 1967.

Wexler, Sanford. *Westward Expansion: An Eyewitness History.* New York: Facts On File, Inc., 1991.

Wright, Louis B. *Everyday Life on the American Frontier.* New York: G. P. Putnam's Sons, 1968.

PRIMARY SOURCE IMAGE LIST

Cover: Photograph of a sod house in Milton, North Dakota, circa 1895, taken by John McCarthy. Housed at the Library of Congress in Washington, D.C.

Page 5: Photograph of crowd waiting to file homestead claims in Perry, Oklahoma, on September 23, 1893. Housed at the National Archives in Washington, D.C.

Page 9: *Map of the United States* by John Melish, 1816. Housed at the New York Public Library.

Page 11: *Daniel Boone,* painting by Alonzo Chappel, 1861. Housed at the Special Collections Research Center, University of Chicago Library, Chicago, Illinois.

Page 14: The Louisiana Purchase treaty, 1803. Housed at the National Archives in Washington, D.C.

Page 16 (left): Portrait of Meriwether Lewis by Charles Willson Peale, 1807. Courtesy of Independence National Historic Park.

Page 16 (right): Portrait of William Clark by Charles Willson Peale, 1807. Courtesy of Independence National Historic Park.

Page 18: Engraving of Fort Vancouver, 1850. Housed at the University of Washington Libraries.

Page 20: *Barlow Cutoff,* illustration, by W. H. Jackson, 1865.

Page 21: *Battle of the Alamo,* reproduction of an original painting by Percy Moran, 1812. Housed at the Library of Congress Prints and Photographs Division in Washington, D.C.

Page 25: "On Indian Removal," President Andrew Jackson's message to Congress on December 6, 1830. Housed at the National Archives in Washington, D.C.

Page 26: The Homestead Act, May 20, 1862. Housed at the National Archives in Washington, D.C.

Page 29: Photograph of Daniel Freeman, circa 1904. Housed at the Library of Congress Prints and Photographs Division in Washington, D.C.

Page 31: "Nebraska, the Garden of the West," broadside, 1869, published by the Nebraska State Department of Immigration. Housed in the Rare Books, Manuscripts, and Special Collections Library at Duke University, Durham, North Carolina.

Page 32 (left): Photograph of Benjamin "Pap" Singleton, circa 1880. Courtesy of the Kansas State Historical Society.

Page 32 (right): Undated photograph of a family of black homesteaders in Nicodemus, Kansas. Housed at the Library of Congress in Washington, D.C.

Page 34: Photograph of the Chrisman sisters, taken by Solomon Butcher in 1886. Housed at the Nebraska State Historical Society in Lincoln, Nebraska.

Page 40: Daniel Freeman's patent certificate, dated January 20, 1868. Housed at the National Archives in Washington, D.C.

Page 43: Photograph of homesteader Ephraim Swain Finch, circa 1900, taken by Solomon Butcher. Housed at the Nebraska State Historical Society in Lincoln, Nebraska.

Page 47: Joseph Glidden's patent for barbed wire, 1874. Housed at the National Archives in Washington, D.C.

INDEX

About the Author

Jason Porterfield is a freelance writer who lives in Chicago, Illinois.

Photo Credits

Cover Fred Hultstrand History in Pictures Collection, NDIRS-NDSU, Fargo; pp. 1, 34, 43 Nebraska State Historical Society; pp. 5, 38 © Corbis; p. 9 © The New York Public Library/Art Resource, NY; p. 11 William E. Barton Collection of Lincolniana, Special Collections Research Center, University of Chicago Library; pp.14, 26 National Archives and Records Administration, General Records of the U.S. Government, Record Group 11; p. 16 courtesy Independence National Historical Park; p. 18 MSCUA, University of Washington Libraries, NA4171; p. 20 © Hulton Archive/Getty Images; pp. 21, 29 Library of Congress, Prints and Photographs Division; p. 25 National Archives and Records Administration, Records of the United States Senate, 1789-1990, Record Group 46; p. 31 Digital Scriptorium, Duke University Rare Book, Manuscript, and Special Collection Library; p. 32 (left) Kansas State Historical Society; p. 32 (right) Library of Congress, Prints and Photographs Division, HABS, KANS, 33-NICO, 1-; p. 35 National Archives and Records Administration, Old Military and Civil Records; p. 40 National Archives and Records Administration; p. 44 Library of Congress, General Collections; p. 47 National Archives and Records Administration, Records of the Patent and Trademark Office, Record Group 241; p. 51 © Bettmann/Corbis; p. 52 Minnesota Historical Society.

Designer: Tahara Anderson; **Editor:** Wayne Anderson;
Photo Researcher: Peter Tomlinson